A Status of Adivasis/Indigenous
Peoples Mining Series – 1

GOA

Land, Mining and Indigenous Peoples
An Overview

DISCLAIMER

The author and the editorial collective are solely responsible for the contents of this report. The views expressed in this report do not necessarily reflect the views of institutions who supported the research nor who supported printing.

A Status of Adivasis/Indigenous Peoples Mining Series – 1

GOA

Land, Mining and Indigenous Peoples
An Overview

Sebastiao Rodrigues

A Status of Adivasis/Indigenous Peoples Mining Series – 1 : GOA

Sebastiao Rodrigues

First Published, 2014

ISBN 978-93-5002-273-3

Published by
AAKAR BOOKS
28 E Pocket IV, Mayur Vihar Phase I, Delhi 110 091
Phone : 011 2279 5505 Telefax : 011 2279 5641
aakarbooks@gmail.com; www.aakarbooks.com

In association with
THE OTHER MEDIA
J 139, First Floor, Vikas Puri
New Delhi 110 018
Phones: 011 2854 3372/73, Fax: 011 4237 1129
Email : tom@theothermedia.org

Printed at
Mudrak, 30 A Patparganj, Delhi 110 091

Acknowledgements

The Status of Adivasis/Indigenous Peoples (SAIP) has been an important initiative of The Other Media and All India Coordinating Forum of Adivasis/Indigenous Peoples. It began with a lot of interest and enthusiasm with a wide consultation among activists, scholars and researchers interested in Adivasis/Indigenous Peoples' issues. However, the process seemed to have had its own pace and could not keep up with the expectation of completing the report on time. The present phase of the programme has covered, state-wise, issues of land and mining in the Adivasis/Indigenous Peoples' areas.

This report on mining issues in the Adivasi areas of Goa has been prepared by Sebastiao Rodrigues. We gratefully acknowledge the efforts made by the author and members of the Editorial Collective (EC) in preparing this report.

Members of the EC went through the report and gave their valuable comments and suggestions. We gratefully acknowledge their contribution that was available at every stage of preparation of the report. The efforts of the EC have been untiringly coordinated by C R Bijoy. The reports owe a lot to his relentless efforts to keep in the loop everyone concerned towards producing good results out of the reports. At the level of The Other Media, Ravi Hemadri, who worked as the Executive Director of the organization through most part of the programme serves as a link between the organization and the EC. He continued to coordinate the final editing and printing of the reports. We gratefully acknowledge the role played by both C R Bijoy and Ravi Hemadri.

We acknowledge and thank the Adivasi Academy, Tejgarh, Gujarat, and particularly Prof. Ganesh Devy, for generously hosting in February 2008, a two-day workshop of members of the EC and authors to review the draft reports. We thank the members of the Advisory Board of the SAIP, who with their participation in the first consultation and later whenever called upon, gave their inputs to the reports. Thanks are due to Shankar Gopalakrishnan who meticulously put together statistical data and selected literature for SAIP.

Finally, we would like to acknowledge and thank our funders ICCO, Netherlands, and TROCAIRE, Ireland, who supported the programme right through the last five years. We are grateful to the Foundation for Ecological Security, Anand, Gujarat, who generously supported the printing of the first phase of reports on land. We thank all of them for being patient with this initiative.

E Deenadayalan
General Secretary

Contents

List of Tables and Maps

Preface

Eighty-eight million Adivasis and indigenous peoples live in India—approximately one-fourth of the world's total indigenous population. Historically self-sufficient, forest-based communities with independent cultural identities, they have been subjected to displacement, dispossession and repression for more than a century and are now India's poorest and most marginalized communities. Since the onset of British rule, and in many cases from much earlier, Adivasis and indigenous peoples have been systematically and forcibly dispossessed of the resources of their homelands. In gross violation of democratic practice, social justice and both constitutional and legal requirements, such dispossession continues to this day. It is also the Adivasis and indigenous peoples who have paid the heaviest price for the current neo-liberal globalization policies, with their land, resources and forests taken from them for private capital—in the name of "economic growth."

These larger processes have been accompanied by the erosion and undermining of cultural identities, leading to a loss of cultural moorings and other markers of ethnicity. Less than half of India's Adivasi communities speak their own language. State and private efforts at "mainstreaming" and against indigenous faiths, practices and cultural mores have had a devastating impact.

Such trends have not gone unchallenged. Despite

growing differentiation, ethnicity has emerged as a strong, consolidating force. Many have organized, often with the help of sympathetic outsiders, to fight against their oppressors and struggle for the control over land and other resources, and for local self-government as in parts of Central India. There have been demands for political self-determination and autonomy of varying degrees as in Jharkhand and the northeast. The state characterizes all such struggles as 'Law and Order Problems', and large parts of central India and the northeast are heavily militarized in the name of 'national security'. In other parts too state repression has been heavy and brutal.

Though these processes are well known to many and particularly to Adivasis and indigenous peoples' movements, there continues to be a dearth of knowledge on the overall status of Adivasis and indigenous peoples in India. The struggle-based mass organizations of Adivasis and indigenous peoples in the Indian subcontinent articulated the need to work towards such a task in the late 1990s. The collective process to fulfil this task was launched in 2005.

The Status of Adivasis/Indigenous Peoples is conceptualized as a series of reports on salient themes affecting the lives of Adivasis/Indigenous Peoples. In the first instance, the series focuses on the situation of land and mining in the tribal tracts of the country. We hope that the series will be effective in not only deliberating upon similar themes of importance to the Adivasi present and future, but also help strengthening linkages amongst movements, activists, scholars and all the others who are concerned with the protection of the rights of Adivasis/Indigenous Peoples in the Indian subcontinent.

This series of reports will explore the history, laws, and facts, and describe the struggles while providing an overview of current realities. The main purpose of these reports is to expand linkages and relationships between movements, scholars, and activists so that the future of the political struggles is informed and forward looking.

Author's Note

I acknowledge the contribution in the form of theoretical guidance offered by the late Dr. Bikram Dasgupta of the Department of Chemistry, Goa University, for the past few years; Durgadas Gaonkar, GAKUVED President, who introduced me to the tribal question in Goa in 2004; Ram Velip from Colamb, Sanguem, Goa for his sharp insights into the past; Roland Martins who first introduced the mining issue to me in 1992 with an exposure trip to Sirgao mines, in Bicholim Taluka; Hanumant Parab and Vasudev Parab from Pissurlem Village who re-introduced me to the mining issue in April 2001 and over the years helped me to visit the deep open cast mines of Pissurlem despite sharp political differences; Ramesh Gauns, Br. Philip Neri D'Souza, Rajendra Kerkar, Prakash Paryienkar, Dayanand Gawde and Ulhas Gaonkar for their insights into the struggles since I began to critically look at mining in Goa in 2001; my brother Albert Rodrigues for his continuous solidarity and sometimes even accompanying me on my visits to the mining sites; C R Bijoy for encouraging me to undertake this study; The Other Media, New Delhi for financially supporting this study and Vikas Adhayan Kendra, Mumbai for financially supporting the Goa state level Seminar on 'Land, Mining and Adivasis' in Panjim in 2007 where this study was discussed.

Various people from the SAIP editorial collective offered

valuable comments such as Prof. Gopal Iyer, Prof. Ganesh Devy, Michael Mazgaonkar, Brian Lobo, Shankar Gopalakrishnan, Ajitha Susan George, Deenadayalan and others at the review meeting at the Adivasi Academy, Tejgarh in Baroda, Gujarat in February 2008. Xavier Dias reviewed this study and the author is grateful for his critical comments.

The author was a coordinator of Mand—an Adivasi Rights Resource Centre, An Initiative of Gawda, Kunbi, Velip and Dhangar Federation till November 2010 during which time this study was undertaken. This situation changed in 2013, yet the author shares his gratitude with the group for all the cooperation, support and collaboration extended from the years 2005-2010. The author is currently a doctoral candidate on Fellowship at BITS Pilani, Goa Campus.

It is hoped that this study will promote further action and reflections leading to emergence of intellectual leadership resistant to co-options of the oppressive system in place.

Siolim, Goa, January 2014 **Sebastiao Rodrigues**

Executive Summary

Goa's geography was shaped by the Adivasis, particularly the *Gawdas*. They were amongst the first settlers of Goa along with the Mahars and Khols. With Proto-Australoid racial origins, they trace their origin to the Khunti region of Chotanagpur in Northern India, the homeland of the *Munda* Adivasi people. Originally hunters, the *Gawdas* settled in the dense forests of what is now known as the Western Ghats, probably as early as 5,000 B.C. Plain lands were reclaimed from beneath the Arabian Sea over the subsequent millennia. The movement of sea water was regulated by a complex network of sluice gates all over Goa.

The *Gawdas* relied on an institution of land holding known as the *Gaonkary*. It collectively administered the village's resources; the whole community was the owner of village lands. There was no private property, and all surpluses were distributed equally within the community.

The prosperity of this land attracted a number of people, some of whom came as migrants and were accepted by the community, while others gradually began to establish control over the Adivasis. Though this second group of migrants faced difficulties initially due to the fact that they did not have the skills to cultivate the land, some villages did fall under the control of these marauding violent bands, primarily because the *Gawdas* are mainly non-violent in nature and chose *flight* rather than *fight*. The Brahmins in particular asserted their control over the conquered lands with violence and shrewdness. They then took steps to convert the Gawdas into landless workers in order to ensure a supply of labour for their cultivation. The migrants were then able to legitimize their conquest after the arrival of the Portuguese in 1510; they were unable to secure state support prior to this time.

The arrival of the Portuguese was a major setback to the status of Adivasis, particularly the *Gawdas*. The Portuguese colonial state that lasted in Goa for 451 years had a unique and powerful state formation: its support base came from those very bands who had sought to dominate the Adivasis before colonial rule. These groups were inept at the fine art of ruling and found the Portuguese to be convenient allies. Moreover, Portuguese colonialism contributed further to land alienation from the Adivasis. The *Gaonkary* system was 'formalized' and transformed into the modern-day *Comunidades;* during this process the Portuguese and the migrant settlers succeeded in displacing the Adivasis from membership of these community bodies, thus taking over all legal control of common resources and lands.

After liberation, the upper caste Brahmins got the Adivasis to sign on blank papers under various pretexts and then created documents that would allow them to acquire legal ownership rights after a decade or so. Owing to their inability to understand the legal system of post-liberation Goa, the Adivasis were easy prey for such land sharks. The Adivasis lost not only their private lands but also their temple lands, which formed a large portion of their community lands. Temples that had escaped attention during the Portuguese colonial regime, with huge land areas attached, were targeted and their management was taken over by the Brahmins. Moreover, the mass of Adivasis were not only alienated from their lands but also from state structures. Without education and awareness of their rights, they are headed towards disaster, as new players in the form of real estate mafias have entered the field.

Meanwhile, the Adivasis have also faced land alienation and accompanying environmental, social and ecological consequences as a result of massive mining operations in Goa. Explorations for mining purposes began during the first decade of the 20th century. The Portuguese brought in German geologists to survey for minerals. After three decades of exploration, iron ore, magnesium, silica and bauxite deposits were found in various parts of Goa. Silica and bauxite were found in coastal Goa, while iron ore and magnesium were found in huge deposits in the inland areas. The colonial state began leasing out these lands for mining from 1929 onwards. All the mining leases that were granted in this period were given in the name of Portuguese nationals, Brahmins (Hindus as well as those who had converted to Christianity), Gujarati traders who were Banias and other businessmen who were close to the colonial rulers, multinational companies, etc.

Jawaharlal Nehru, the Indian Prime Minister under whose regime the Indian army launched 'Operation Vijay' and captured Goa within two days in December 1961 after delaying to do so from 1947, entered into elaborate negotiations with these mining lease holders before taking the decision to send the Indian army into Goa. It is only after he entered into a secret pact with the mining lease holders and mine operators, which guaranteed that the Indian government would extend the mining leases granted by the Portuguese colonialists, that Nehru mustered the confidence to enter Goa—a full 14 years after the British had left India. Such was the power that these groups collectively wielded over the state structures in Goa.

Most of the land under mining leases is forest areas where Adivasis have lived for thousands of years. Adivasis have faced two processes that have resulted in them losing these lands. On the one hand, mining leases are active in many such areas, while on the other, large tracts of forest have been declared to be wildlife sanctuaries. These areas include the Bhagwan Mahavir Wildlife Sanctuary, Bondla Wildlife Sanctuary, Mhadei Wildlife Sanctuary, Netravali Wildlife Sanctuary, Khotigao Wildlife Sanctuary, and Salim Ali Bird Sanctuary. The Adivasis living inside these sanctuaries are subjected to various kinds of restrictions by the Forest Department.

Protests against mining have intensified since 2007. There have been various instances of direct people's occupations of mines in Sanguem and Quepem talukas. The police and the administration have inevitably tended to side with the mining companies, and people have been subjected to various repressive measures. This has also been the case with the protests against SEZs and industrial estates, most of which have also come up on Adivasi lands.

The liberation of 1961 was in reality the liberation of the elites of Goa. These elites, who gained this status precisely by robbing the Adivasis of their lands and resources, now enjoy power and continue the exploitation. For Adivasis, the struggle for liberation is just beginning. These elites are Brahmins. They are racially different from the Adivasis as well as Mahars and share the qualities of being cunning and aggressive to establish their control over land by illegitimate and fraudulent means.

1

Introduction

Till very recently few people were aware that there are Adivasis in Goa. Apart from anthropological surveys, little data was available on Goa's Adivasi population. The information on their struggles was even scarcer, with no written history available. There are several reasons for this. Goa received international attention only after the 1960s, when the tourism industry sought to market Goa as a tourism destination. Unlike other parts of India, the Adivasis of Goa took *flight* into the interiors of the dense Western Ghats forests rather than *fighting* when faced with external threats. Consequently, the Adivasis of Goa, especially the Gawdas, also spread out into the border districts of South Karnataka.[1] The other major Adivasi group, the Dhangars, migrated frequently, crisscrossing the borders of Goa, Karnataka and Maharashtra. It is only in the recent past that they have stabilized their habitations in Goa. The struggle of Goa's Adivasis since 1961 has also remained disconnected from

1. Some of the villages founded by the Gawdas after their *flight* from Goa includes Gall, Vaspad, Kubgall, Amball, Lande, Landavaddo, Kellimollo, Nuzi Patnem, Hulvi Patnem, Baradi, Bhalpoll, Kundal, Kelleli, Kuralli, Ghottavar, Navar, Kashingall, Athrem, Bhairem, Kalle, Marconni, Bhizolem, Bargta, Kotem, etc.

the wider Adivasi movements in India. The Adivasi leadership of that time deliberately confined the movement to within the boundaries of Goa.

This study is not intended to be the final word on the subject, but rather is a snapshot of my understanding of the Adivasi situation in Goa. This has developed ever since I was introduced to the process in late 2004, through the eighth annual conference of Nature Environment Society and Transformations (NEST) on 'Indigenous People' in Ranchi, Jharkhand. This was also the first time that Adivasi movements in Goa were connected to wider movements in India. Representatives of the Gawda, Kunbi, Velip and Dhangar Federation (GAKUVED), representing Goa's Adivasi groups, participated in this meet and interacted with groups in Jharkhand and other parts of India. This interaction led to the beginning of a slow process of conscientization on the land question amongst Adivasis in Goa.

1.1 The Silence on the Struggles of Adivasis in Goa

There is very little literature available on the history of the Adivasis of Goa. One of the few works available is a pioneering study by Vinayak Khedekar, *Goa Kulmi: Paryavarniy Sanskritiche Janak, Rakshak* (Goa Kulmi: Nurturers and Protectors of Environmental Heritage), written in Marathi and published in 2004.[2] Though this work touches on various aspects of Adivasi life, its focus is largely cultural, and it does not discuss the question of land and mining. The book also does not deal with the Dhangars.

Indeed, studies on Dhangars, or Goulies, as others call them, are even scarcer. A study by Bernadette Gomes is yet to be published. And most rare of all is to find works by Goa's Adivasis themselves. Adivasis are more adept at oral narration of their history and identity than the written with

2. Self-Published, 2004. Panaji.

exceptions of Surya Gawde[3] and John Fernandes[4] who attempted to do this process in written form. This situation is understandable, as the Adivasi communities possess an oral tradition rather than a written one. It is only those schooled the Western educational model who develop the capacity to write in English. Considering the high drop-out rate and lack of inclination to pursue higher education, any change in this situation is unlikely in the near future without organized efforts.

This study attempts to throw some light on the changes that took place in the Adivasi land relations during Portuguese colonialism, as well as subsequent developments that affected these land relations. The focus here is on the Gawdas and excludes Dhangars due to my lack of exposure to them. The study is the outcome of my first hand experience with the Gawda, Kunbi, Velip and Dhangar Federation (GAKUVED), and interactions and reflections with many people, largely the common people collectively engaging in reflecting on their past while shaping and constructing their future.

1.2 The Traditional Adivasi System of Resource Control

Goa's geography was shaped by Adivasis, particularly the Gawdas. They were amongst the first settlers of Goa along with the Mahars and Khols. With proto-Australoid racial origins, the Gawdas trace their origin to the Khunti region of Chotanagpur in Northern India, the homeland of the Munda Adivasi people. Originally hunters, the Gawdas settled in the dense forests of what is now known as the Western Ghats, probably as early as 5,000 B.C. Rock carvings on the banks of Kushavati river in Rivona in South Goa belong to this period. At that time, there were no plain lands

3. Gawde Surya, *Silent Goa*, Human Resource Development Trust, Ponda, 2009.
4. Fernandes, John, *Goycho Mull Avaz*, GPL Prakashan, Quepem, 2013.

Map 1: Settlement Pattern of Scheduled Tribes in Goa

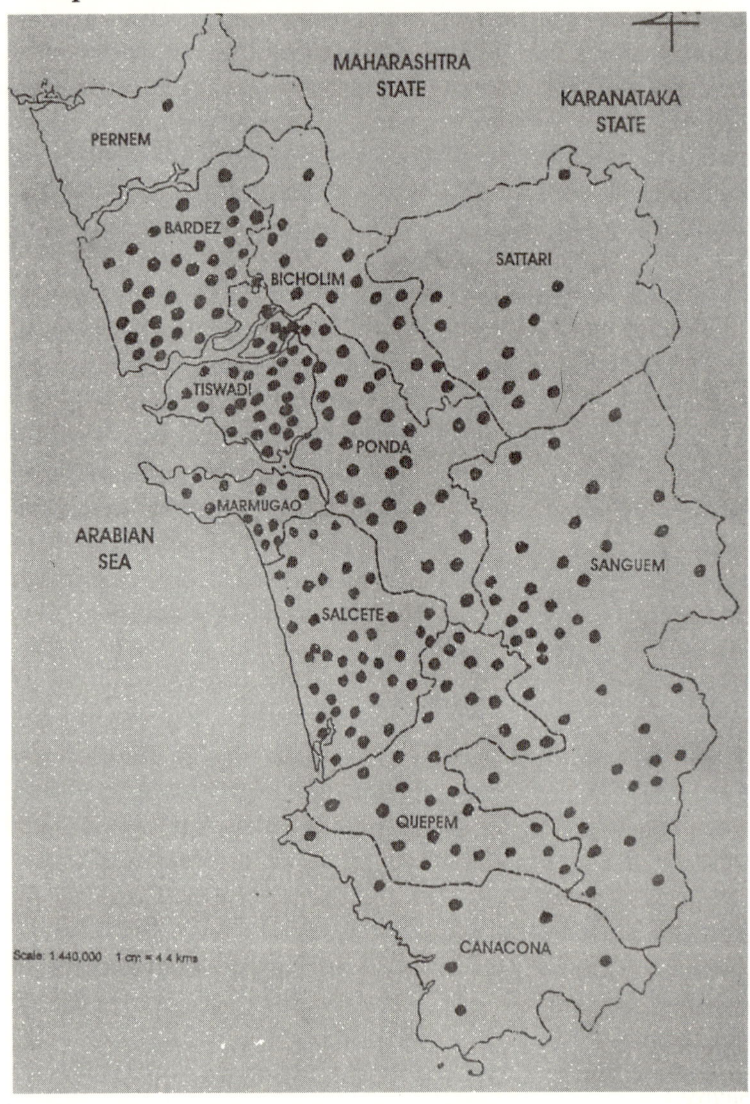

in Goa. The Arabian Sea extended up to the base of the mountains. The plain lands one finds today were reclaimed from beneath the Arabian Sea over the following millennia. The movement of sea water was regulated by a complex network of sluice gates all over Goa. This network regulated the water flow during the high tide and low tide, creating predictable water flow and allowing the rest of the land to be brought under cultivation of various kinds, such as rice and coconut, in varied cultivation forms such as *Bhatam and Kulagaram*. Some of the wild trees, such as jackfruit, were also domesticated and cultivated.[5]

Goa, known by various other names as Gopakkapattnam, Goavapuri and Gomantak, became very prosperous, becoming the envy of many, who now sought to establish their rule over the Adivasis of this region.

Table 1: Scheduled Tribe Settlements in Goa

Sr. No.	*Talukas*	*No. of ST Villages*	*Total ST Population*
North Goa =123 Settlements			
1.	Tiswadi	31	20,755
2.	Bardez	33	2,647
3.	Pernem	01	36
4.	Bicholim	16	5,080
5.	Sattari	12	4,159
6.	Ponda	30	29, 622
	Total	123	62,299
South Goa = 136 Settlements			
7.	Salcete	41	37,453
8.	Marmugao	12	8,301
9.	Sanguem	43	15,602
10.	Quepem	30	25,396
11.	Cancona	07	13,005
	Total	133	99,757
Grand Total		256	162,056
Total Scheduled Tribe Settlements in Goa = 256			

Source: Goa State Commission for Backward Classes, *Survey Report on the Scheduled Tribes of Goa (Gawda, Kunbi, Velip)*, Directorate of Social Welfare, Government of Goa, Panaji, Goa, February 2004. The twelfth taluka of Darbandora was not yet demarcated from Sanguem taluka at that time.

5. Discussions with Ram Velip of Colamb, Sanguem, Goa in 2007.

Goa's hinterlands and hilly regions were converted to cultivation. Natural water flow was carefully observed over generations and cultivation was organized as per the land gradient.[6] Rice and other vegetables were cultivated during the non-monsoon season inside fresh water rivers like the Mhadei; this form of cultivation was called *Puran Sheti*. The soil was specially prepared for the purpose and cultivated year after year. Paddy fields were established on the banks of rivers, depending upon the landscape. Rice and other vegetables would be cultivated twice a year as *Rabi* and *Kharif* crops. In some places, only one crop a year was grown. *Khazan* lands, adjacent to salt water rivers, are also reclaimed lands that act as a buffer between the mainland and salt water rivers. *Kulagars,* next to paddy fields, were horticultural spice gardens. Later, betel nuts, pineapples and sugarcane also came to be cultivated in the *Kulagars*. Further inland, the *Bhat* lands were predominantly used for coconut plantations. Further inland lay the *dongar*, the mountains. On the mountains too there are cultivation spaces, the *Kumeri,* for crops that do not require a large quantity of water.

Thus, tremendous labour has gone into shaping Goa's geography and making it both habitable and prosperous. This was only made possible by the innovations of the Adivasis and the tremendous spirit of cooperation within their communities.

1.3 Adivasi Institutions of Governance

The Gawdas evolved social institutions for the governance of their community and its resources. Two institutions played a crucial role in this. The first was the *Mand*. It is the oldest social institution in the area, established around 5000 BC.

6. The order of cultivation was pointed out by Venkatesh Prabhudesai of Quinamoll, Colamb, Sanguem, Goa in 2007 to the author in a private interview. He is a Brahmin and owns large tracts of land in Colamb, Sanguem taluka.

One can know the history of the *Mand* only through the oral tradition, as no written records exist.

The *Mand* used to be an open space, sometimes with trees like Banyan, Pipal and other forest trees, situated in the middle of the village, and ranging from 20-25 square metres to 5,000 square metres. Beneath this tree one can find a small stone structure called *Ghumti.* There is no idol kept in the *Ghumti. Mand* is also found among Catholics in the *Gawda* community.

The same term, *Mand,* was then used to describe the body elected by the community during its assemblies in this space. All those who attain the age of 18 years can be members of the *Mand.* A member who is over 65 years old is exempted from membership and becomes a duly respected elder. Social, cultural, religious, political and economic decisions are taken in the *Mand.* The head of the *Mand* is called *Manda Guru.* His position is supreme.

The *Mand* looks after the problems relating to the land in the *Gaonkary* system, under which all land was held in common. The *Gaonkary* system played a significant role in controlling and administering all the land that belonged to the *Mand* as per oral rules and regulations, including those being used for agriculture, horticulture, and grazing, as well as forest lands. The concept of private ownership did not exist.

Adivasi communities are emotionally and spiritually at one with nature, as is evident from their rituals, some of which are documented in *Goa Kulmi: Paryavarniy Sankskritiche Janak, Rrakshak.*[7] The Gawdas in particular are pioneers in founding and administering villages. They derive the name Gawda chiefly from this function; *Ganv vosoupi ani ganv gaddo choloupi ho Gawdo* goes the saying in *Konkani,* meaning 'Gawda is the one who founds and administers the village'[8].

7. Vinayak Khedekar, 2004.
8. I have learnt this from Durgadas Gaonkar.

1.4 The Entry of the Migrants

The prosperity resulting from the landscaping and transformation created by the Adivasis attracted migrants, some of whom the community accepted. Others, however, gradually sought to take control over community lands, converting Adivasis into labourers.[9] Their methods included raiding of communities and forcible takeovers of community lands. The invading communities included Brahmins and others like Ranes of Sattari taluka. Very often these tactics did not work, as communities abandoned their villages and fled to new areas in the forest, founding new villages. The invaders did not possess the skills to cultivate the land as the Gawdas had done. Hence, they had to arrange labour from the Gawdas from some other village to cultivate the conquered villages. This was not easy as each village would have their own cultivation to undertake.

Despite these difficulties, some villages were brought under the control of the violent bands of migrants, who seized large tracts of land. This occurred chiefly because the Gawdas are non-violent in nature and chose flight rather than fight in response to the attacks. The shrewd Brahmins asserted their control over the conquered lands violently. However, they were not able to legitimize their conquest till the arrival of the Portuguese in 1510, as they lacked a formal alignment with state power before that year. Recent scholarship has demonstrated that Brahmins, like the Portuguese, share foreign origin. This explains as to how Brahmin-Portuguese collaboration ensured Goa's colonial rule lasted for 451 years.

---

9. My discussions with Ram Velip of Colamb, Sanguem, Goa.

2

Portuguese Colonialism and Adivasi Land Alienation

Pressure from the migrants on Adivasi lands, particularly of the Gawdas, intensified with Portuguese colonialism and the patronage of the new rulers. Portuguese colonial domination lasted for 451 years. Its main support base came from the very marauding bands who had sought to dominate tribes prior to colonial rule, but who did not have the art and skills to rule—the Brahmins. They found the Portuguese to be convenient allies.

2.1 Creation of Private Bhatcars

The control and legal transfer of land from the Adivasis to Portuguese nationals and Deshprabhus, Prabhudesais and Ranes, and later on Dempos, Salgaonkars and Chowgules; commenced with the aid of the Portuguese rulers. Conversion to Christianity, the faith propagated by the Portuguese colonizers, was one method adopted for the smooth grabbing of land of the Adivasis. Largely it has been observed that the Adivasis who are converted to Christianity do not have land in their possession and are therefore forced to function as a stock of labour supply to the landlords who are Brahmins. These Brahmins need not be of the same village but it could be some other distant village. The example of Nesai village in Salcete that is re-named during Portuguese rule as Sao Jose de Arial is largely an Adivasi village of those converted to Christianity but the land is owned by the Brahmins settled in Curtorim village of Salcete taluka. Some of the migrants even changed their names and surnames to Portuguese, becoming metaphorically white to different shades. Others colluded with the Portuguese without converting to Christianity.

These migrants came to be known as Bhatcars meaning landlords. The absence of any previous written documents further aided the transfer of lands. The Portuguese colonial State, with the stroke of a pen, created written documents granting legal ownership to these land usurpers. The colonial police and military were at the service of these new landlords who prospered under Portuguese colonialism, learning Portuguese and becoming part of the colonial administration. Once they had joined the administration, creation of land records in their names was even easier, and they walked into the post-liberation era as the dominant and affluent class.

As a result, the colonial era saw large tracts of land being parcelled out to private individuals, mostly Brahmins, who in fact constitute less than 2% of Goa's population. Consequently, they have been able to politically and economically dominate the rest of the population, even 50 years after the so-called liberation in 1961. In fact in 2013 it can be safely said that Goa is under the colonial rule of Brahmins of various shades like Saraswats, Karade, Chitpavans, etc.

2.2 The Role of the Colonial Church

Portuguese colonialism also sought to transplant the faith of the colonizers onto the colonized. European religious traditions were super imposed on Goa, which was transformed into a major centre for the spread of Christianity in Asia. The colonial strategy of using religion as a part of conquest contributed towards the capture of Adivasi lands.

Adivasi places of worship were demolished in large numbers and replaced with churches. Though these shrines have often been described as Hindu temples, they were not. In fact, *'Hindu'* as a defined religious category was yet to emerge during the early Portuguese colonial period.[10] Rather, caste categories were in currency. The colonial Church was controlled directly by the Crown in Lisbon and locally supported by the Bhatcars. Indeed, converted Brahmins and non-converted Brahmins shared a common interest in these activities as a result of their class and caste affiliation. It was in their interest that temples be demolished, not so much for religious reasons as much as to take control of the lands that the temples controlled.[11]

Hence, large tracts of community lands under temple control were taken over during these demolitions, especially from 1510 to 1610, the first 100 years of Portuguese colonial rule. The temple committees did not offer much resistance to the marauding bands in alliance with the Portuguese colonizers and fled with their deities. This process of appropriation continued for four centuries, as a result of the alliance between the colonial rulers and the upper caste migrants.

Mass conversion of Adivasis and bans on pre-conversion rituals, seeking complete adherence to the new faith, were imposed by the colonial agents in charge of the villages,

---

10. Sammit Khandeparkar at the history seminar at CES College, Cuncolim on March 13, 2007.
11. In fact, Sergio Mascarenhas, a Portuguese historian presently heading Fundacao Oriente in Goa, claims that Goans themselves were responsible for the temple demolitions during Portuguese colonial rule. The word 'Goan' is problematic as it conceals the heterogeneous nature of society, projecting everyone, the oppressors and the oppressed, as a single category. The question here is: which Goans were involved in breaking down of temples? These claims were made at a discussion on this theme at a History seminar in CES College, Cuncolim held on March 13-14, 2007.

known as *regidors*. These conversion drives very often consisted of throwing pieces of bread on the roof tops of houses and into the village common well and declaring that whoever was staying in the house and whoever drank the well water would be deemed to be converted. They were then to report to the church the next day and get their new faith, name and surname.[12]

Such strategies also extended to attempts to wipe out the Adivasis' own faith. The Adivasi deity is known as *Devchar,* having neither form nor shape, but organically tied with nature and the members of the Gawda community. *Devchar* was the most powerful spirit and symbolically protected villagers and their lands. *Devchar* was also known as *Rakhandar* or *Ajoba,* and is said to reside in the *Raim* or sacred grove.

Devchar became the target of attack and denigration by Brahmanical forces and the Church authorities. The Church authorities translated the word 'Devil' as '*Devchar*' when writing in Konkani. As a result, the theological contest in Western Christianity between *God* and the *Devil* was translated as a contest between *Dev* and *Devchar*. Brahmanical forces in turn termed *Devchar* as '*daitya shakti*', meaning evil force, that ought to be eliminated from the face of the earth. Symbolically, the Adivasis had to be robbed of their powerful defensive symbols that marked their spiritual relationship with their ancestral domain, in order to make them defenceless and demoralized during the colonization and seizure of their community lands.

Thus, alienation from land was combined with alienation from their faith and culture. The Brahmins, in collusion with the colonial powers, the Church and Christianity, consolidated their control and domination. In the language of Church discourse Adivasis are classified as pagans that were in need of conversion. But even after conversion the

12. My discussions with Durgadas Gaonkar.

new found faith of Christianity did not empower them to take control of their land and reduced themselves subservient to the Brahmin landlords. Church in its turn had done nothing during the colonial era as well as post-colonial era to dismantle the system of landlordism, instead cemented this system by glorifying it till landlords went on a spree of sale of land displacing the Adivasis of their habitats, livelihoods and cultivation spaces.

Besides owning land at village level, the Church also took over lands through an institution called Santa Monica. Santa Monica became the legal owner of vast lands from all over Goa, including the grazing lands of Adivasis. The takeover of grazing lands of Dulapem village in Tiswadi Taluka is one such example. The Church sold this land to the multinational company CIBA-GEIGY that is currently known as Syngenta at a throw away price after the liberation of Goa. The corporate, as a mark of gratitude to the church, named its factory as 'Santa Monica plant'. Goa's Catholic church is the biggest landlord in the State of Goa, next only to the State-owned lands according to Fr. Dr. Victor Ferrao, a Catholic priest teaching at Rachol Seminary.[13]

2.3 Formation of 'Communidades' and the Suppression of 'Gaonkary'

The colonial rulers also undertook efforts to destroy the system of Adivasi community institutions described in the previous section. The Portuguese started a process of registering the '*Gaonkaries*' and requiring them to have written rules and regulations, imposing an alien system on the traditional system of resource control and, in most cases, initiating the process of land alienation. The colonizers began referring to the *Gaonkaries* as *Communidades*. The registration process was used by the migrants to take control of the community lands held by the *Gaonkaries*. As a result, out of

13. Presented at the seminar held on June 22-23, 2013 at Pedro Arrupe Institute, Raia, Salcete, Goa.

around 220 registered *Communidades,* barely two had some representation from the Adivasi communities. The rest were registered under the names of the marauding bands who had taken over Adivasi lands. These included Brahmins, many of whom made false claims that the *Gaonkary* system was theirs. After the *Gawdas* were alienated from their system, these *Communidades* functioned without them, keeping meticulous written details of the genealogy of their members and annually collecting their share of income (known as *Zon).* The *Communidade* institution was mainly administered with the objective of providing legal evidence that those whose names were written in the *Communidade* records were the original holders of these lands. Hence, over time, the *Communidades* degenerated. The foundational principle among Gawdas for the governing of these lands was deep internal solidarity and a strong spirit of cooperation, both of which were lacking among those who had seized control of the *Gaonkaries.* Having been deprived of their lands, the Gawdas were then reduced to being a reserve force for labour, especially on the farmlands parcelled out to the supporters of colonial rule in Goa. They were also denied education during colonial days, which was largely reserved for Brahmins. The rule of Manusmriti did not vanish from Goa even during the times of Portuguese colonialism. Discouraging of students from the communities from those other than Brahmins is just one example of this grim reality. The destruction of the *Gaonkary* system and its replacement with the *Communidades* completed the alienation of Adivasi lands.

2.4 Creation of the Mokaso System and Adivasi Land Alienation

Portuguese colonialism expanded to the full territory of Goa in phases. The first few islands to come under Portuguese occupation were Divar along with Zuem in Tiswadi Taluka. Soon after that, Tiswadi Taluka as a whole came under Portuguese rule. The next phase of expansion took place in

Bardez and Salcete talukas. These areas are known as old conquest areas. Inquisition policies and conversions were made fully applicable to these talukas of Goa first, during the first 250 years of Portuguese rule. The next phase of expansion was in Quepem, Pernem, Bicholim, Sattari, Sanguem, Ponda and Canacona talukas. These places were under the rule of different dynasties before the Portuguese arrived. The colonizers entered into a series of diplomatic and military negotiations with the dynasties in order to bring them under Portugal's rule as vassals or tributaries. One common understanding in the case of all these negotiations was restraint in implementing conversions and inquisition policies. Each of these areas was then subjected to particular conditions in regard to payment of taxes to Portugal and compliance with Portuguese laws.

One set of conditions was imposed as part of a pact with Rane warriors. The Ranes were appointed to collect taxes on behalf of the rulers of Sawantwadi in Maharashtra, known as Sawants. However, for various reasons, the Sawants conceded their territories in Goa to the Portuguese, and the Ranes were left without a job. Trained in warfare, they decided to launch an attack against the Portuguese rulers in a bid to pressure the colonial state into an agreement that would ensure the protection of Ranes and also grant them additional privileges. After a brief war that included guerrilla fighting in the forests of Sattari and Bicholim talukas, the Ranes entered into a settlement with the Portuguese. Under the settlement, the Ranes were to halt their attacks. In return, the Portuguese would give additional privileges to the Ranes in the form of *Mokaso* lands in Sattari and Bicholim talukas. These lands in fact belonged to the Gawdas, but as a result of this agreement, they were legally transferred to the Ranes in Sattari and Bicholim talukas. All together five such tracts of land were gifted to the Ranes. The lands were located at Advai, Khadki and Saleli in Sattari taluka, and Sankhelim and Maulingem in Bicholim taluka.[14] The identity of Ranes is still unclear. Claims are being made that they are Marathas. There are other claims that maintain that they are Brahmins. The behaviour of Ranes in post-colonial Goa, especially of the former Chief Minister Pratapsingh R. Rane, in protecting the Brahmanical system, allowed his constituency of Poriem to be badly ravaged by the mining industry. The cultivators, the Gawdas who had in fact created these fertile lands, were nowhere in the picture as far as the legal record was concerned, but they continued to work on these lands. The dominant position of the Ranes got consolidated in Sattari and Bicholim talukas during Portuguese rule. The Ranes also made efforts to establish their own kingdom in these talukas. Fear amongst the Gawdas and the introduction of a feudal ethos led to increased exploitation of the Adivasis. Liberation for the Ranes came to mean liberation from the obstacle that Portuguese control posed to their efforts to establish their own rule.

14. I have learnt this from Durgadas Gaonkar and Dayanand Gawde.

3

Liberation of 1961: What It Meant to Adivasis

With Nehru's decision to march militarily into Goa, the Portuguese alliance with Goa's mining industry and dominant castes was over. The mine owners' secret understanding with Nehru, based on which the Government of India allowed the leases to continue, meant that the mining industry would come to play the key role in the formation of the state in post-liberation Goa. This is reflected in the fact that most Chief Ministers of Goa, after its liberation, were engaged in the mining business. For the first 20 years of its existence, the State was ruled by a mining baron, Dayanand Bandodkar, and his daughter Shashikala Kakodkar. Pratap Singh Rane, whose roots lay in the colonial system of *Mokaso,* ruled for the following decade, and was then repeatedly brought in as a 'consensus' Chief Minister during the subsequent 20 years of political instability. Meanwhile, the legal infrastructure created during the Portuguese colonial regime continued to guide post-liberation Goa till 1987.

The Adivasi situation did undergo some changes after 1961. The first Chief Minister of Goa took progressive steps in two sectors: education and land reforms. Marathi medium schools were set up all over Goa, and some Adivasi children were able to receive education at these schools. Many

Adivasis however continued to provide cheap labour, sometimes even free labour, to Bhatcars and *Mokaso* owners. Desais and Bhats (Brahmins) intensified their pressure on the Adivasis and gradually tricked the Adivasis into transferring the Adivasi lands into their names. Under various pretexts, Adivasis were persuaded to sign on blank papers, thereby creating documents that would give the Desais and Bhats ownership rights after a decade or so. Unable to understand the legal system, the Adivasis fell prey to land sharks. Not only were the private lands taken out of Adivasi control in this fashion; the Adivasis also lost their remaining temple lands. Temples with huge lands that had escaped the attention of the Portuguese colonial regime were targeted and their management was taken over by the Brahmins. The Mangueshi temple in Ponda taluka and Malkhazan temple in Canacona taluka are two of the best known examples. In the case of Malkhazan, the Brahmins even changed the temple's name to Mallikarjun temple[15] in order to Sanskritize the name and erase its Adivasi roots. In other cases, Adivasi deities such as *Paik Dev* were subjected to vandalism in Sanguem taluka.

3.1 Bhatcars v/s Mundcars

Only a small minority amongst the Adivasis were able to take advantage of the *Mundcar* laws that provided security to those living in land owned by Bhatcars. Such persons were given the name Mundcars. The Mundcars were supposed to enter into litigation against the Bhatcars in order to receive ownership of the piece of land where their houses were located. Their entitlement was 300 square metres of land, which of course amounted to only a small portion of the lands

15. Vinayak Khadekar has dealt with this trend of taking over of tribal community lands and temples in his book in Marathi called *Goa Kulmi: Paryavarniy Sanskritiche Janak, Rakshak* that he self-published in 2004.

that had been taken over. In practice migrant settlers from other parts of Goa, brought in by the Bhatcars as labourers, became the main beneficiaries of the *Mundcar* laws. Those Adivasis who had continued to stay on in their original homes had stayed there on the condition that they would supply labour to the Bhatcars to cultivate their coconut and betel nut orchards. The Bhatcars adopted various methods to discourage such Mundcars from sending their children to schools. They argued that the children of Mundcars needed no education as they would still be needed to provide manual labour to the Bhatcars. After a few years, such children were and continue to be pulled out of school, usually at the primary school level. The result is that many Mundcars do not know that they have a claim on the lands that they reside on. Many continue to live at the mercy of the Bhatcars.

This is a particularly severe example of how the Adivasis have not only been alienated from their lands but also from State structures. Without education and awareness of their rights, they are headed towards a dire situation, particularly with new players in the form of real estate mafias entering the field.

Meanwhile, the Adivasis' status has worsened in *Mokaso* lands. The Ranes often deny Adivasis entry to these lands, which were made cultivable only by the hard labour of their ancestors. Sometimes they are not even allowed to reside and work there as labourers for anything more than a short period, due to the fear that they may make a legal claim on the lands. Further, the *Mokaso* system has exacerbated land alienation, and in fact perpetuated the hegemonic position of Ranes in Sattari and Bicholim talukas. On December 28, 2005, there was a revolt in Saleli village and one of the male members of the Rane family was stoned to death in broad daylight by the villagers, who were protesting against various forms of feudal domination.

Table 2: Land Ownership Among the Scheduled Tribes in Goa

Scheduled Tribe	*Agricultural Land (In Hectares)*				
	Land Owned	*Land Taken On Lease*	*Leased Out*	*Kumeri*	*Land Total*
Gawda	10,089.73	1,835.91	6,538.28	862.38	6,249.75
Kunbi	280.99	121.65	3.50	18.46	417.60
Velip	2,823.92	415.90	14.36	246.65	3,472.11
Total	13,194.64	2,373.46	6,556.14	1,127.49	10,139.46

Source: Goa State Commission for Backward Classes, *Survey Report on the Scheduled Tribes of Goa (Gawda, Kunbi, Velip)*, Directorate of Social Welfare, Government of Goa, Panaji, Goa, February 2004.

Table 3: Housing Status of Scheduled Tribes in Goa

Sr. No.	Scheduled Tribe	*Residential House*									*Total*
		Own			*Rented*			*Mundcarial*			
		Pucca	*Semi-Pucca*	*Kacha*	*Pucca*	*Semi-Pucca*	*Kacha*	*Pucca*	*Semi-Pucca*	*Kacha*	
1.	Gawda	5,440	14,366	2,906	123	349	142	447	2,882	1,290	27,945
2.	Kunbi	252	592	223	10	17	9	5	78	30	1,216
3.	Velip	1,277	3,534	1,536	41	47	20	5	33	44	6,637
	Total	6,969	18,492	4,765	174	413	171	457	2,993	1,364	35,798

Source: Goa State Commission for Backward Classes, *Survey Report on the Scheduled Tribes of Goa (Gawda, Kunbi, Velip)*, Directorate of Social Welfare, Government of Goa, Panaji, Goa, February 2004.

Table 4: Household Basic Amenities Among Scheduled Tribes in Goa

Sr. No.	*Scheduled Tribe*	*Power Supply*		*Drinking Water Facilities*			*Source of Energy for Cooking*				
		Electrified	*Not Electrified*	*Tap*	*Well*	*Others*	*Electrified*	*Firewood*	*Gas*	*Kerosene*	*Others*
1.	Gawda	26,903	1,042	17,361	8,916	1,668	63	21,560	5,272	1,039	11
2.	Kunbi	1,123	93	654	346	216	4	925	266	21	0
3.	Velip	5,751	886	3,573	1,628	1,436	6	6,368	206	55	2
	Total	33,777	2,021	21,588	10,890	3,320,	73	28,853	5,744	1,115	13

Source: Goa State Commission for Backward Classes, *Survey Report on the Scheduled Tribes of Goa (Gawda, Kunbi, Velip)*, Directorate of Social Welfare, Government of Goa, Panaji, Goa, February 2004.

4

Mining and Minerals in Goa

Explorations for mining purposes began in Goa during the first decade of the 20th century. The Portuguese brought in German geologists to survey for minerals. After three decades of exploration, iron ore, magnesium, silica and bauxite deposits were found in various parts of Goa.[16] Silica and bauxite were found in coastal Goa, while huge deposits of iron ore and magnesium were found in inland areas. The colonial state began granting mining leases in the 1940s. By the end of the 1950s, about one thousand mining leases had been granted in the talukas of Sanguem, Quepem, Bicholim, Sattari, Bardez and Pernem. Actual mining operations began in 1945, and the first 100 tonnes of iron ore were exported to Japan in 1948. This ore played a crucial role in the recovery of the Japanese economy, which was in a state of collapse after the nuclear attacks by the USA in 1945. Goa remained Japan's chief supplier of iron ore and magnesium until recently, when exports from Brazil replaced Goan iron ore.

Bicholim and Sattari talukas were among the first areas to lose their paddy fields, forests, mountains, ground water and livelihood support systems to the mining industry. Most of these lands originally belonged to the Adivasis. Moreover,

---

16. See mining lease Map of Goa.

aside from the lands taken for the mines themselves, the onset of mining in a non-mechanized form triggered off internal migration within Goa. Adivasis as well as non-Adivasis were drafted to work in the mines. The migrant workers settled in the area, but did not own lands in the mining villages; this laid the seeds for future confrontations[17] with the Adivasis who were attached to those lands.

Two rivers, Zuari and Mandovi, began to be used to transport the ore to Marmagaon Harbour. From the harbour, the ore would be loaded into large ships for export to Japan. The waves caused by the movement of the ore-carrying barges in the rivers damaged *bunds*[18] in adjacent riparian island villages, like Divar, and often led to minor floods.

During colonial times, all the mining leases that were granted were in the name of Portuguese nationals, Brahmins (including those converted to Christianity), Gujarati traders and other businessmen who were in the good books of the colonial rulers, multinational companies, etc. These were precisely the elements that enabled Portuguese colonialism to continue its rule for an additional 14 years after the rest of India had attained independence. In fact, Jawaharlal Nehru, the Prime Minister under whose regime the Indian army launched 'Operation Vijay' and captured Goa in December 1961, had entered into elaborate negotiations with these mining lease holders before taking the decision to send the Indian army into Goa. He agreed to a secret pact with the mining lease holders-cum-mine operators, under which the Indian government committed to respect the mining leases granted by the Portuguese. It is only after this was agreed that Nehru mustered the confidence to enter Goa. Such was the power that the mine owners collectively wielded over the State structures in Goa.

17. This situation is visible in Colamb village in Sanguem taluka.
18. Bunds are barricades that block the entry of saline water into paddy fields. They were constructed by the Adivasis while claiming lands from the bosom of the Arabian Sea many thousands of years ago.

In fact, a few years before 'Operation Vijay', T.B. Cunha[19], a stalwart among freedom fighters against Portuguese colonialism, wrote in a Mumbai-based journal titled *Free Goa* that it was the mining companies that were responsible for perpetuating Portuguese colonial rule in Goa. In the article, published in 1958, he said:

> 'The main cause of the failure to liberate Goa even ten years after the independence of India is the systematic sabotage, carried by Indian businessmen against all the efforts made by Goans and by others (sic) to achieve the liberation. This is now clear to all those who have studied the Goa question objectively and do not believe in the lame excuses invented to explain the shameful continuation of the occupation by Portugal of territories situated in India. It is not the lack of unity among Goans nor the lack of co-operation on the part of Indian people to achieve integration of Goa, Daman and Diu into India that is responsible for the indefinite postponement of freeing them from foreign rule. It is the protection given by some Indian politicians in power to the Indian businessmen for carrying a profitable speculation in Goa with the full connivance of the Portuguese officialdom. That mainly is responsible for the present state of affairs.
>
> The facilities given by the Portuguese government to the Indian businessmen are such that they have made them interested in the continuance of Portuguese rule in Goa and made them wish to postpone as long as possible the liberation of the Portuguese occupied territories. The Indian politicians who support these Indian merchants do not seem to realize that the profits made by them are gained not only at the cost of economic and financial interests of India, but are also detrimental to her national unity, territorial integrity and future security. Narrow-minded and unable to grasp the national interest, they believe that the profits made by Indians

19. Cunha, T.B., *Portuguese Occupation of Goa Supported by Indian Merchants*, in *Free Goa*, July 25, 1958, reproduced in Tombat, Nishta, *Tristao De Braganza Cunha (1891-1958) and the Rise of Nationalist Consciousness in Goa*, Appendix three, Ph.D. dissertation, Goa University, Goa, 1995.

compensate the country for the loss it suffers otherwise from Portuguese occupation.

We have repeatedly shown here, giving names and figures, that the help given by Indian capitalists to exploit the Goan mining wealth has served to increase the revenue of the Portuguese administration and to allow it to maintain an army of many thousands of European and African soldiers and officers and a costly political force. The exploitation of the mining industry and the contraband trade which is simultaneously carried on by the same Indian traders is the main source of income to the Portuguese in Goa who themselves have not invested a single rupee in our country. Under the camouflage of a fictitious economic blockade and sanctions, which they have sabotaged, the Indian merchants, together with some foreign speculators, have extended to the Portuguese the help they needed to perpetuate and consolidate their domination in Goa.

In addition to the help given for the extraction of the iron and manganese ore, the Indian Capitalists have also helped the Portuguese to improve the transport of the minerals by railways, roads and rivers, to build a new and big airport and to extend the works of the Marmagao (sic) harbour. We have given here the names of Indian businessmen including Goans who have invested their capital in all these concerns. Some of these persons are known to be well-related with Indians and some foreigners. The capital, the management and even a great part of the labour is Indian and are closely connected with concerns functioning in India.

A further contribution to help the Portuguese fo consolidate their position in Goa is now the formation of a ship-building society with the co-operation of the Indian capitalists who run the mining industry and indulge in its complementary smuggling trade. The capital subscribed to the new society comes from the Government of Portuguese, India and other institutions depending on the government which are compelled by the government to lend their funds. But a good amount of their capital is also brought by the Indian and foreign firms working in Goa. The capital invested by Private Indian and foreign concerns is indeed superior to the sum invested by the government.

The following is the list of the Indian and foreign investors who have contributed to the funds of new society and who also permanently co-operated with Portuguese in strengthening foreign hold on Goa. Here are the most important names:

Chowgule and Co. Ltd.
Damodar Mangalji and Co. (India) Ltd.
Gangadhal Agrawal
Hiralal Khodidas
Khantilal & Co. Ltd.
Mineira Nacional Ltd.
Subraya & Co.
Timble Brothers Ltd.
V.M. Salgaonkar & Brothers Ltd.
V.S. Dempe & Co. Ltd.
Joao Hogo Sequira
Madev Sinay Talaulikar
A. Abdulrazak
Sesa Goa Ltd. (Germano-Italian)
W.I.P Railway (British)
Mingoa society (Italian)

The installation of the ship-building works is to be started in Vasco da Gama near Marmagao harbour under the direction of Portuguese, Indians and Britishers. The capital subscribed amounts to nearly 35 lakhs divided in shares of Rs. 100/- each. The report accompanying the project of the Ship-Building Society clearly says that it aims at resisting India's efforts to unite Goa to India. It has not prevented the protégés of our Congress patriots to fully co-operate with the Portuguese in the anti-Indian endeavor. They may allege that it is "constructive work" (Gandhian terminology) pursued by Indians in Goa with the connivance of pseudo-Gandhians in power in India. As a matter of fact they are plundering and mortgaging Goan wealth for the immediate benefit of Portugal.

While the Indian government is quietly awaiting to settle the problem of Goa by "peaceful negotiations" the Indian moneybags are allowed to peacefully help the Portuguese and enrich themselves at the cost of the Indian and Goan economy, of the suffering Goans and non-Goans and more than anything else, at the cost of Indian national integrity, her good name and her safety. It is in the interest of these moneybags indeed that the settlement of the Portuguese pockets has been postponed indefinitely. They are the people who spread false and distorted news about Goa and mislead and misinform the official circles in India about the real situation of Portuguese territories in India. Only the Indian Government must understand that they are not interested in the liberation of Goa because when it comes, it will deprive them of their easy and tainted profits. One must also know that these double dealers are the real political informers and advisors of the Portuguese on the Goan question.

One must say that these unscrupulous merchants would not have succeeded in their treacherous work of support to the foreign occupants of Goa if they had not received all facilities from Indian authorities to carry on their nefarious activity. Not only they were given in India all normal facilities allowed to honest traders but they were left free to act in contempt of law and resort to criminal corruption to carry on their smuggling activities which are complimentary to the Goan mining industry. In fact, since independence they were treated as a privileged class allowed to prosper at the cost of the most vital interests of the nation. Before the relaxation of the permit system when common people were harassed in every manner when they had to travel to and from Goa, it was precisely these merchants for whom the economic restrictions really meant (sic) who enjoyed all sorts of facilities thanks to powerful friends they had in the official circles. No wonder that the supposed economic sanctions failed miserably and some had to be removed as ineffective. In fact, they are sabotaged in benefit of these unpatriotic citizens and lawbreakers.

While our brave Goan and non-Goan liberators were facing by hundreds and thousands the most fascist repression of the Portuguese Police State, suffering long years of prison, deportations, beatings, tortures and even death, these Indian adventurist traders were amassing fortunes and prospering at the expense of other people's sacrifices. And it is precisely these people who are now carrying the whispering campaign against Goans accusing them of being responsible for the failure of liberation because of the lack of unity between their too numerous political parties. As a matter of fact, the disrupting activity among Goans and non-Goans was the work of these very slanderers of the Goan movement who infiltrated bogus nationalists in the ranks of our workers or corrupted others with their tainted money. The whispering campaign is meant to cloak the guilt of those who are really responsible for the continuance of the foreign domination in apportion of the Indian land even after independence. But their treason shall not remain concealed or forgotten."

This article provides a brilliant glimpse of how mining companies relied on the Portuguese colonial state as their protector. The Indian state allowed these leases to continue, and they were eventually formalized when the government of Goa enacted the Goa Daman & Diu Mining Concessions (Abolition and Declaration as Mining Leases) Act 1987. This law declared that the leases granted by the Portuguese stood abolished and all such leases would instead be deemed to be mining leases granted under the Mines & Minerals (Development & Regulation) Act 1957. This is by virtue of the provision contained under Rule 24 A (9) of Mineral Concession Rules 1960.[20]

Major changes did, however, occur in the wake of 1961. First, mechanization of the mining sector began after Goa's integration with India. Moreover, the mining companies used the Indian state in a radically different manner than the way they used the Portuguese colonial state. Adivasi land alienation in Goa must be looked at in this context of these developments and changes in the international political economy.

4.1 Mining and Adivasi Land Alienation

The talukas of Sanguem, Quepem, Sattari, and Bicholim are rich in iron ore deposits and have been the site of open cast mining during the past half a century. These two talukas are full of mining leases granted during Portuguese colonial rule, which were then renewed under Indian laws.

---

20. According to the reply furnished under the Right to Information Act to Motesh Antao of Colomba, Rivona, Sanguem dated April 23, 2007 by A.T. D'souza, Senior Geologist, State Public Information Officer, Department of Mines and Geology, Government of Goa.

Deep craters dot the landscape. Massive destruction of agriculture due to mining silt deposited in the agricultural fields, acute water shortages, widespread lung diseases such as tuberculosis due to dust pollution, high rate of accidents due to plying of mining trucks, drying up of natural springs, damage to houses due to explosions, and displacement of people from their fields and residences owing to rapid expansion of mining to newer areas are some of the consequences. Socially, hatred and disharmony have spread as mining companies have engineered divisions and conflicts amongst the villagers. Some of the longer term problems include destruction of forest cover, depletion of marine wealth due to the release of silted water in the fresh waters of rivers, decline in crops due to lowering of ground water, and destruction of natural sponges that retain rain water and recharge aquifers. State agencies have shown apathy and indifference in taking action against mining companies, even as the police have provided them with security in the face of popular discontent.

The Centre for Science and Environment's sixth report on the State of India's Environment, titled *Rich Lands, Poor People: Is "Sustainable" Mining Possible?*[21] makes this important observation about Goa:

> Goa is India's smallest state—spread over 3,70,200 ha, it accounts for just 0.11 per cent of India's geographical area. It is however, one of India's leading producers of iron and manganese: four per cent of India's iron ore reserve and eight per cent of its manganese ore reserve are in Goa. In 2004-05, more than 15 per cent of iron ore produced came from Goa.

21. Published by the Centre for Science and Environment, Delhi, 2008. The title of the book has the word sustainable in inverted commas. This has *Tadi par* implications, suggesting that sustainable mining is impossible—which has been the experience of the communities in the mining belts across India for over the past 100 years. *Tadi Par* as concept, text and context is dealt with in greater depth in Rodrigues, Sebastiao 'Tadi Par as Development Metaphor: Experiences From Goa', 2008.

> The state has about eight per cent of its total area under mining, the highest in the country. Some 400 mining leases have been granted in Goa till 2002-03, covering approximately 30,325 ha—this works out to almost five per cent of the total area leased out for mining major minerals in the country. Of these, 222 mining leases have been granted for extracting iron ore: this account for 56 per cent of the total area under mining.

The book further states that:

> The value of mineral production in Goa, which has continuously increased since 2000-01, stood at Rs 829 crores in 2004-05; iron ore accounted for 99 per cent of this value...the state contributed one per cent of the value of minerals produced in the country.
>
> But the mineral royalty received by the state government was a pittance—Rs 15 crores, Rs 18 crores and little more than Rs 17 crores respectively in 2002-03, 2003-04 and 2004-05. Revenues from mining account for a miniscule 0.8-1 per cent. While private miners are making windfall profits, the government and the people of the state are seeing none of it.

The book has an interesting account of the history and political economy of mining in Goa:

> The history of mining in Goa is intrinsically linked with its colonial past. When the Second World War ravaged Japan, leaving its economy in shambles, the country needed iron and steel to rebuild itself. Goa, with its huge reserves, was well suited to meet this demand. Portugal realized that this market was a potential gold mine, and decided to tap it. Portugal also realized that it needed to involve some local Goans and people from other Portuguese colonies in its plans; like all colonisers, it hoped that these agents would support its regime in order to protect their own interests. In fact, Chowgule and Dempo, who have huge stakes in Goa's mining industry today, were migrants who worked for the erstwhile Portuguese dynasty.
>
> Following this strategy, Portugal awarded mining leases in perpetuity to some Goans—mainly small businesspeople. Ever since, large-scale mining of iron ore and its subsequent hugely profitable export has been an integral part of Goa's economy and society—leaving an indelible impact on Goan society and

> environment.
>
> It is also a colonial legacy that mining in Goa is still largely in private hands, even after the liberation of Goa and its integration into India. After the Indian Army took over Goa, the mine owners went to the International Court of Justice at Hague, which was to decide whether Goa was 'Captured or Liberated'. The Indian government agreed to let it be termed 'liberation', and this gave rights to the mine owners to carry on with the mining concessions granted by the Portuguese. In 1986, the concessions were abolished and converted into leases, which were deemed granted.

This was the historical process by which Goa was punished with *Tadi par* by mining companies. Exploitation and usury are the hallmarks of this industry, which has created a concentration of political power in the hands of a few mining companies.

There is a further reference in the report on mining's impact on other communities:

> Unrestrained iron ore mining has devastated the lifeline of Goan society—its farmlands, forests, rivers, air and ground water—and Goa's people are feeling the pinch. Most mines in Goa work below the ground water level. About 10 tonnes of water have to be pumped out for every tonne of ore mined. This leads to depletion of ground water in the surrounding areas. Surface water from the rivers also seeps and flows into the mining pits, leading to drying of the river downstream.

4.2 Resistance to Mining

Protests had begun against the mines during the Portuguese era, but records of these protests are difficult to trace. The earliest recorded protests took place in 1964 in Colamb village in Sanguem taluka. A Bhatcar, on whose land Adivasis were employed, had approached government authorities and the courts against the mining lessee. Subsequently, a private agreement was reached between the lessee and the Bhatcar. A translation of this agreement is included in the box below. The document is interesting for two reasons: first, the land originally belonged to the Gawdas; second, the document clearly indicates the nature of the mining problems being faced by communities, and the manner in which local non-mining elites reacted.

On 10th September, 1964, in this New Town of Curchorem, there appeared as FIRST PARTY Hiralal Khodidas, married, merchant, residing at Cacora, and as SECOND PARTY Vassudeva Rama Boto Colombkar, married, landlord residing at Colomba, Taluka of Sanguem, and they agreed as follows:-

1. *That the first party is the grantee of iron oxide and manganese mine denominated "GOGORO" or "GULCONDA DONGOR", situated at Colamba.*
2. *That adjacent the said concession lie the properties denominated "TOLEM" and "MALVADEM", attached among themselves, of plantation of coconut trees, areca nut trees and other fruit yielding trees, belonging to the said second party Colombcar.*
3. *That due extraction of ore and its transport from the referred concession has caused damages in the said properties such as accumulation of sterlites, perishing of coconut seedlings due to the crossing of trucks etc.*
4. *That by the present agreement the damages caused so far have been computed to one thousand rupees, which sum the second party received from the first party, in this act, and he gives him the necessary discharge thereof.*
5. *That the said first party promises to pay to the said Boto, annually, the sum of Rs.50/- till the end of May of each year as compensation towards the damages that may be caused in future to the second party due to the exploration of the said concession; and in the event it is needed to fell any fruit yielding trees, they already fix up to Rs.100/- for each palm tree, Rs. 5/- for each cashew nut tree of less than 3 years of age, and Rs. 10/- for each cashew nut tree more than 5 years of age.*
6. *That the second party commits himself from today to relinquish from complaints or any inspection requested to the Directorate of Agriculture and to the Civil Judge of the Sub-District of Quepem. The first party obliges himself to pay the costs of the preventive measures which have been taken by the referred Civil Court.*
7. *That the said first party obliges himself to pave with paving*

stones the way that crosses the aqueduct and to elevate the way at other places to prevent the loss of water.

8. *That the first party obliges to refrain himself from burning any product in the property, in which event he shall pay damages towards the perishing of trees.*
9. *That the second party shall freely utilize the roads made by the first party.*

In witness thereof the present agreement has been drawn up, which after having been read and found accordingly is going to be signed by the parties and by the witnesses present. The original copy bears the court fee stamp of one rupee and ten paise, being one rupee towards the agreement and the rest towards the discharge.

(Sd/-)
Vassudeva Rama B. Colombcar
Hiralal Khodidas
Inacino Diniz
Mahasukal Jamaldas

It is clear from this private agreement that mining was negatively affecting local people. However, the Bhatcars in the village treated this problem as purely a question of damage to what they regarded as their property, and sought compensation for themselves alone. Having received cash and access to roads built by the company, they withdrew their complaints. The Bhatcars did not consult any other section of people in reaching these 'agreements', not even the Adivasis whose land it originally was. Nor did they seek to actually reduce the damage caused by mining. As a result, the problems remained and pollution continued to haunt the village. The only difference after the private agreement was that there was peace between the mine operator and the landlord, both of whom would now share the earnings from mining, though in highly unequal proportions. Moreover, the landlord could act against the mining operator even to this extent only because he also belonged to a class of exploiters, and hence was educated and aware of the functioning of the State. The mass of people were not educated in 1964, nor was there any movement among Adivasis on the land and mining issues then.

Map 2: Mining Lease Map of Goa

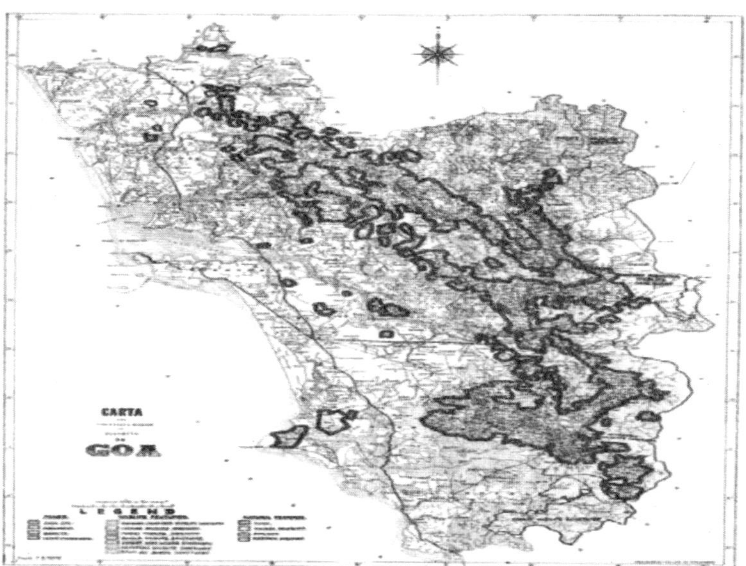

Source: Department of Mines and Geology, Government of Goa, Panaji, Goa.

Most mining leases fall within forest areas. The alienation of these areas from Adivasis has taken place both as a result of these mining leases and through the declaration of other forest areas as wildlife sanctuaries. Goa has a number of wildlife sanctuaries such as Bhagwan Mahavir Wildlife Sanctuary, Bondla Wildlife Sanctuary, Mhadei Wildlife Sanctuary, Netravali Wildlife Sanctuary, Khotigao Wildlife Sanctuary, and Salim Ali Bird Sanctuary. Adivasis living inside these sanctuaries are subjected to various kinds of restrictions by the Forest Department. One Adivasi was even shot dead by the forest guards while collecting fire wood inside the Khotigao Wildlife Sanctuary in Canacona taluka in South Goa some years ago. In spite of the tyranny of the Forest Department, Adivasis continue to reside on forest land in most of the sanctuaries, though in the Bhagwan Mahavir Wildlife Sanctuary the Forest Department relocated a few

Map No. 3

Source: Alvares and Saha, *Sweet Land of Mine*, Goa Foundation, January 2008.

villages and paid them monetary compensation (no alternative land was provided). The Forest Department prevents Adivasis from catching forest crabs and harvesting mushrooms in the name of forest protection, even as it turns a blind eye to the damage caused by mining activities inside the sanctuaries.

Large-scale mining took place in 2006 and 2007 in the Netravali Wildlife Sanctuary, with the active collusion of the Forest Department. Well known companies like Dempos, Timblos, etc routinely violate State laws and get away scot-free, even as they expand mining deep in the most dense forests and release silt in the nearby rivers. Sivsorem Dempo mine in Sanguem is an example of such violations, where mining has resulted in the village lands drying up. The government is now working towards supplying water to the village from the nearby Salaulim dam, whose reservoir in turn houses another mine, in this case operated by the Timblo mining company. The water that the villagers will get, which also supplies the cities of Margao and Vasco, will hence be polluted with high doses of chlorine and potassium permanganate. Timblo's mine has been inspected by a number of state agencies, including the Governor of Goa M.C. Jamir. Yet this mine continue to operate with scant regard for the law and the health of the people.

The Sivsorem case is only the tip of the iceberg as far as Goa's mining scenario is concerned. No accurate figure for the number of existing mines or the actual area under mining in Goa is forthcoming from the State authorities. While the Portuguese had given out 808 mining leases for iron ore and magnesium, the total area leased is still to be calculated; alternatively, if it has been calculated, it is not being revealed. However, in a reply to a Right to Information query in 2007, the Department of Mines and Geology[22] stated that the 'total area covered by 439 mining concessions is 30,646.26 Ha and the total area of 15 leases granted under the MMDR Act 1957

22. In the reply from K.M. Hegde, Assistant Public Information Officer, Department of Mines and Geology, dated June 6, 2007 under the Right to Information Act 2005 to Rama L. Velip of Colomba, Rivona, Sanguem, Goa.

is 2403.50 Ha.' What happened to the remaining leases? Have they not been included in the department's statistics as they are within wildlife sanctuaries? Can it really be true that only 15 leases have been granted all over Goa under the MMDR Act? Does this mean that the remaining mines are operated illegally? If yes, then why had they not been closed down and the violators punished? It does seem from the above reply that the rest of the mines are operated illegally.

Pissurlem Mining Protests

It is only in the last decade that the seeds of a movement on land and mining have gradually begun to form. The Adivasi movement in Goa had earlier focused on the demand for their recognition as scheduled tribes (STs). The Scheduled Tribe status was eventually extended to Gawdas, Kunbis and Velips in 2001. The Dhangars were tricked out of this and their struggle continues. The land question, however, largely remained neglected in these struggles.

One example of the developing contemporary movement is the protests against mines in Pissurlem village. The mines in this settlement in Sattari Taluka are half a century old. Adivasis live here along with other later settlers, especially the Parabs, who control Pissurlem Communidade. Dalits too live in this village. Over the past 50 years, almost every family in the village had lost either their homes or their agricultural lands. The village supplied labour, including women, to the mining companies during the era of non-mechanized mining. However, over the years, after the village was displaced twice, protests have gradually mounted against mining. First, the protests came from the Parabs against silting of agricultural fields. Pissurlem had recorded the highest rice yields in Sattari taluka until the late 1980s, when mechanized mining began leading to silting of agricultural lands coupled with acute water shortages. Mechanized mining also intensified the problem of mining waste, or overburden as it is otherwise known. The Pissurlem *communidade* eventually took action against illegal dumping by mining companies in the communidade lands. Gradually, other communities, including Adivasis and Scheduled Castes, joined the protest. In one letter[23] to the government agencies, they jointly carried out an audit of the destruction in the village by the mine.

It says, '*The mining operations which is presently going on in the vicinity of our village panchayat areas have already seriously undermined the integrity of our watersheds, disrupted ground water aquifers and tables, destroyed paddy fields, disturbed wildlife and degraded habitat of us. Most of the ore rejects have descended and every time with rainy season, descending with the rains into our rivulets, creating their own brand of havoc.*

The mining entrepreneurs always give tall promises but on many occasions, we personally have experienced that these promises are hardly met by them. We have been so fatally assaulted that presently never be able to rehabilitate again. The larger volumes of ore excavated have created in their wake a number of mind boggling environmental problems for which at present there is no cure. The mining ore rejects have choked up extensive areas of tanks, fields, nallahs and riverbeds and in some areas rice fields are now one metre higher than they were earlier, being completely filled with mud from mining dumps and pits. Due to mining activities functioning in undemocratic manner, our life has become veritable hell... nothing indigenous grows here, and slopes are routinely prone

---

23. Dated November 14, 2003 and addressed to the member secretary, Goa State Pollution Control Board objecting proposed extraction of Iron Ore at T.C. No. 70/51 and 2/Fe/71 of village Panchayat Pissurlem. This is signed by 23 villagers from Pisssurlem: Hanumant Chandrakant Parab, Pundalik Tulshidas Parab, Shiva Ramchandra Chari, Somenath Sitaram Pawar, Anand Navaso Gawde, Shivanand Tulshidas Parab, Ramesh Tulshidas Parab, Shankar Narayan Parab, Balchandra Gawde, Pratap Gawde, Tulshidas Vishnu Gawde, Anant Khapulo Gawde, Radio Sasro Gawde, Narendra Gamba Gawde, Rajendra Arjun Gawde, Nanshiv Uttam Gawde, Dhasu Jaganath Gawde, Babuso S. Gawde, Shashikant Dholo Gawde, Hari R. Gawde, Premnath R. Gawde, and Pandurang V. Porob.

to landslips posing danger to the people of the area. At many places vast areas have been converted into heaps of mining waste. We are ultimately getting dust and diseases. Hardly, we get fresh air and clean water. Use of explosives too, is causing huge cracks in several houses. This is a regular phenomenon.

Whatever arguments, views expressed by the applicants, namely R.S. Shetye and Damodar Mangalji and Co. are hiding reality and misleading in the copies of the executive summary in form XIII filed by them. We do not trust both the entrepreneurs due to the bitter experiences. They have already destroyed our agriculture and allied activities and put us into a tight corner threatening our sources of livelihood and also making our future bleak.

Hence, we earnestly urge you not to grant permission for the proposed expansion of mining industry unless and until all our above referred grievances are settled in right earnest.'

This is yet another example of increasing resentment over mining. This was, however, not the last, as a number of protests later erupted all over the inland areas of Goa in the wake of the Government of India's moves to increase mining clearances during the second phase of liberalization. Sattari's Sanvordem and Gavanem villages successfully held mining companies at bay. Sarvan village too saw an intense movement against a mining company in 2007. In Sanguem taluka, protests are gradually taking on a mass form after the successful protest by Colamb villagers in 1981.[24]

Colamb Mining Struggle[25]

Colamb village has very complex dynamics. It is an almost unique case of an Adivasi village in Goa that negotiated with both Brahmins and the Portuguese, without great loss of land

24. Got to know this from Ram Velip from Colamb in June 2007.
25. This case study was made during June 5-13, 2007 at Colamb and neighbouring villages of Sanguem and Quepem along with Devidas Gaonkar from Bordem, Khotigao, Canacona, Goa.

to either of them. It is also a village that the Portuguese paid special attention to, and for which they framed special notifications dealing with land and village deities.

Colamb is among the oldest Adivasi settlements in the area. The inhabitants are Gawdas and have 'Velip' as their surname. Their population had increased and new houses were constructed in nearby lands during the pre-colonial days. Even after the arrival of the Portuguese, Sanguem came under their control only two centuries after they had begun taking over other parts of Goa. By that time, the Dessais had begun to settle in the village, seizing Adivasi lands by the use of force. The Gawdas had their own system of governance before the arrival of the Portuguese. This was known as the *Bodvont* system, in which the village head was known as the *Budvont*. *Budvonts* of different villages together formed a body that settled the affairs of the community across villages. This body had its own meeting space, with a special seating arrangement consisting of stone chairs.

The Dessais, in collusion with the Portuguese colonial regime, got themselves included in the community's systems for the governance of land affairs. First, they got themselves included as members of the Colamb communidade, though —unlike almost all other settlements in Goa—in Colamb the Adivasis managed to retain control over village lands.

Besides entering the communidades, the Dessais also got themselves notified[26] as co-founders, along with the Gaoncars and Velips, of the local temple. This temple is located at the centre of a large area of Adivasi land.

However, for the cultivation of their farms, the Dessais needed labour—in particular Adivasi labour, as no one else had either the necessary skills or the Adivasis' honesty and unmatchable dedication to work. Hence, the Dessais brought in new workers from other Adivasi villages, who were then settled in Colamb village. The Dessais then tried to culturally

26. *Boletim Official do Governo do Estado da India*, Sabbado 1 de abril, Anno 1882, No. 36.

integrate with the Adivasi migrant workers. They organized their *Mand* to include participation from Adivasis along with the Dessais. Various Adivasi festivals were then started in the *Mand,* such as the joint celebration of the prominent festival Shigmo. Indeed, Colamb may be the Adivasi village where the Dessais and Adivasis celebrate Shigmo jointly and have a common *Mand.* Shigmo is entirely an Adivasi festival, of the Gawdas, and the *Mand* is exclusively their institution. The Dessais engaged in this action in order to tie the Adivasis to themselves completely, culturally and symbolically, in order to ensure continuous supply of labour for themselves and for future generations of landowners. The Dessais have succeeded in this endeavour chiefly because they have ceaselessly employed Adivasis on their lands and ensured that their children do not go to schools and get formal education. The Dessais' sole aim has been to get steady, stable and reliable supply of Adivasi labour across generations.

Through such methods the Dessais accumulated a huge amount of surplus capital, which is now invested in mining and anywhere else that the opportunity arises. On the other hand, the workers that work in these farms—*Kulagars* and *Bhatams*—live a hand-to-mouth existence; many of them cannot even think of opening a bank account. This however is also due to the fact that Adivasis do not possess the concept of saving for tomorrow or of investment. Traditionally, Adivasis would share any surplus with the entire community. Wealth is thus continuously re-distributed amongst the entire community. This generates balance in levels of prosperity and does not allow for stratification and the growth of inequality in their community. These are not the ethics of the Dessais. They exploit Adivasi labour to the maximum, earn as much as possible through sale of produce and then re-invest the surplus in buying more lands, starting new businesses, and in providing the best of education to their children and to those of their community.

Colamb has huge deposits of iron ore and manganese. Under the Portuguese colonial regime, the entire village was divided into various leases, and if all of them were now to be activated, the village itself would become a story of the past. Attempts were made to start mining in Colamb village during the Portuguese regime on an experimental basis. The damage was not major, as it was the era of hand mining and mechanization had not set in.

Meanwhile, during roughly the same period, the entire Adivasi population living in the forest lands around Colamb was wiped out by small pox, with only one person—who had come to live in the plains lands—surviving. It is indeed mysterious that a small pox outbreak hit the village as soon as it was discovered that the village had mineral deposits. One is reminded of the Native Americans in North America, who too were hit by small pox and tuberculosis epidemics, mainly in the mining localities, leading to a drastic decline in their population. This was due to the European colonial strategy of biological warfare, aimed at finishing off indigenous populations and getting unhindered access to the wealth of the 'new world', which lies in the minerals under its soil. One wonders if a similar strategy was adopted by Portuguese colonizers with the aid of their supporters in Goa in order to clear the way for accessing minerals.

The sole survivor of the smallpox epidemic was also the *Budvont* of the village, an adopted boy from an Adivasi family from the neighbouring village of Cazur in Sanguem taluka. However, he proved to be a chronic gambler and unable to manage the village lands. It was his son who showed an interest in cultivation, and the entire village lands were gifted to him, for him to pass on to future generations. This land too was targeted by the mining companies and mining commenced. It was in the early 1980s that the villagers, now much greater in number, again began battling miners and forcibly stopped mining. One of the villagers, Rama Velip, was imprisoned for a day and released. He is not aware of the further details of his case as his lawyer began to side with the mining company and the files have remained with the lawyer. Despite this, Rama Velip, along with his brothers and family members, dumped mining waste into the mining pits and managed to undertake cultivation on the resulting lands. This comes across as the first struggle among Adivasis in Goa against the mining giants.

After liberalization, however, newer challenges emerged. In 1990, the village was inhabited by the original Adivasis, the Dessais, the migrant Adivasis who had been brought in to work in the farmlands of Dessais, and other migrants brought to work in the mines during the 1950s in the mines. After manual mining was stopped, these workers' children and succeeding generations settled in Colamb; taking up various jobs in and around the village. In the second phase of liberalization, when mining activity greatly expanded, mining companies have found this category of people to be useful allies at the ground level.

The most controversial mine that has been stopped by the villagers' resistance is on land leased out to Hiralal Khodidas and is operated by the Fomentos mining company. The successors of the former mining workers had meanwhile taken over the leadership of Colamb Panchayat as well as the contract to operate the mine. The seed of confrontation lies precisely here; this section did not possess any agricultural land in Colamb and therefore had no attachment to the village. They used their positions of power to quickly accumulate wealth and drive themselves out of hunger and poverty. But the mining that is their chosen method of doing so is impoverishing other people—the Adivasis of the village. The resulting confrontation has been playing up in Colamb village since 2007.

This contradiction has united the rest of the villagers against the mine: the original Adivasis, because they stand to lose most directly in case mining becomes a reality; the Dessais, because their farms are going to be affected due to water depletion; and the migrant Adivasis, because they are dependent on the farmlands of the Dessais some of whom are Marathas and others Brahmins. In the resulting battle, ranged on the one side are those with bonds to the land:

emotional and livelihood-based in the case of the Adivasis of both kinds, and on the other, economic-commercial interests in the case of the Dessais. Ranged on the one side are the mining companies, the emerging mining mafia, and on the other the descendants of mining workers who hope to benefit monetarily from mining operations. The police side with the mining company, and indeed it was the police who illegally cleared thick forests in 2003 to clear the way for mining projects.

Mining has spread beyond Colamb to nearby villages, leading to protests there as well. In Muscavrem, tribals began protesting in 2003 against a mine operated by Timblos. After two years, the protest fizzled out and the mine started in full swing. The leaders of the movement were co-opted by various perks such as cash and trucks to operate. In Sulcorna village, protests are ongoing. The Salgini village, near the Karnataka border, in Sanguem taluka has also been up in arms. In Tudov, there was a protest in 2003 and mining was halted. Other mines in the area were stopped after the Goa Foundation filed a case in the Supreme Court against mining within sanctuary areas. However, in 2007, preparations were on again to start mining in forest areas. New roads were created by mining companies by clearing forest lands, resulting in massive deforestation.

The people of Vichundrem village filed letters of protest in January 2005 against attempts at activating an old mining lease[27] in their village. However, in spite of this, a contractor was employed to clear forests on village land. The contractor was an Adivasi from Colamb village and was given the task of breaking the villagers' unity. First, he built a temple for the villagers. The villagers, who are a mix of Adivasis and other communities, accepted the temple but refused to let the mining take place in the village. As a symbol of protest, they blocked the road made for mining purposes with a huge boulder.

27. T.C. 38/52 of Hiro Bombo Gauns.

Protests against mining intensified in Goa since 2007. There have been various instances of direct occupations of mines in Sanguem and Quepem talukas. The police and administration have inevitably tended to side with the mining companies and people have been subjected to various repressive measures.[28] Meanwhile, mining companies were operating a large number of mines in the Bhagwan Mahavir Wildlife Sanctuary, the Mhadei Wildlife Sanctuary and the Netravali Wildlife Sanctuary. A petition by the Goa Foundation in the Supreme Court led to the stoppage of around 80 of these mining leases. The mining companies then approached the Supreme Court seeking permission to resume mining in 65 leases inside sanctuaries; but they lost this case.

The years 2007 to 2012 marked the intensification of the protest movement with litigations against the mining companies in the Goa bench of the Bombay High Court, mostly argued by the Goa Foundation, an NGO that aligned with the protest movement. Mining companies retaliated with filing of nearly 700 criminal cases against people involved in the resistance movement across the State of Goa. Most of these cases were concentrated at the police stations at Quepem and Bicholim. Sebastiao Rodrigues, the author of this report, was tagged as a 'Naxalite' by the then leader of the Goa Legislative Assembly and current Chief Minister Manohar Parrikar in 2008 and a defamation suit worth Rs. 500 crores was filed against Sebastiao Rodrigues at the Calcutta High Court citing loss of mining contracts due to his writing online at www.mandgoa.blogspot.in. The lawyer defending the accused villagers in criminal cases, Advocate John Fernandes, was charged with attempt to murder by a policeman attached to the Quepem police station in

28. Detailed documentation of various protests around mining issues in Goa till 2010 is available at blog: www.mandgoa.blogspot.com. The online documentation of protest from 2011 onwards is available at www.bharatmukti.blogspot.in.

December 2008. Protests attracted national and international attention, and the meeting held in London with the banks funding Vedanta mining company in 2009. The loud voice emanating from Goa finally compelled the central government to include Goa within the scope of the Commission headed by Justice M.B. Shah that was set up by the union government via gazette notification dated November 22, 2010.

The Shah Commission report on illegal and irregular mining in Goa was tabled in the Indian Parliament on September 7, 2012. It duly recognized the sufferings tribal communities in Goa have been confronted with due to the reality of mining activities. In addition, it calculated that Goa's mining has caused a scam of nearly Rs. 35,000 crores. It examined every mine in Goa on a case by case basis and marshalled evidence to prove that every mine operating in the State of Goa is illegal and named 153 people responsible for the same including government officers and politicians such as Chief Ministers and Mines ministers from the years 1994 till 2012.

The reports of the contents of the report that was made public by the government via internet evoked wide publicity in the media. In order to cash in on the publicity, the Goa government issued a temporary order suspending all mining operations in the State of Goa as the Goa government is committed to zero tolerance to corruption. Goa Chief Minister even declared that his government will register an FIR against earlier Chief Ministers such as Digambar Kamat and Pratap Singh Rane of the Congress Party. No such FIR has been registered by the state government till July 2013.

Central Minister for Environment and Forests, Jayanti Natarajan, declared on September 12, 2012 that environment clearance granted for 93 mining leases in Goa would be suspended within a few days and it was done so. This was done after the Shah Commission report indicted the Ministry of Environment and Forests in facilitating and abetting various legal violations.

There was hectic lobbying from the mining industry at this juncture to patch up political differences between the BJP and Congress and to re-start mining. It was a popular perception that the mining in Goa is halted only temporarily because of opposing parties are in power at the State and Centre— BJP in Goa and Congress at Centre (Delhi). AITUC, a Trade Union, was in the forefront along with mining industry to vociferously ask for resumption of mining.

In the middle of all this, the Goa Foundation approached the Supreme Court based on the Shah Commission report. The matter came up for hearing on October 5, 2012. The Supreme Court directed the Centrally Empowered Committee (CEC) to investigate into Goa mining affairs and report back within four weeks. Along with this, the Supreme Court directed that all the mining operations of the leases identified in the Shah Commission report and transportation of iron ore and manganese shall remain suspended.

CEC submitted its interim report to the Supreme Court on December 7, 2012 further indicting the mining industry. The Supreme Court refused to revoke suspension of mines. The case is being heard in the Supreme Court.

4.3 Industrialization at the Cost of Adivasi Lands

Besides mining, most of the industrial estates that have come up in Goa were created on traditionally Adivasi lands. In some cases, these were *Kuala* lands, in others grazing and agricultural lands. The industrial estates completely changed the function of these lands, denying access to traditional cattle grazers and sealing the area off with compound walls and, at times, even with barbed wire. Though the Adivasis had lost legal control of these lands during Portuguese rule, they were still performing an agrarian function, even if the resulting surplus was taken by the Bhatcars. The entry of industry created a completely alien system for the Adivasis. It took almost a decade before they were able to adjust and apply for unskilled low paying jobs in the industries.

The creation of these industrial estates took place without any protest precisely because they were being installed on Adivasi lands. The Adivasis meekly surrendered their lands to the estates and also for mega projects such as a chemical plant of the Swiss multinational Ciba-Geigy at Corlim, Tiswadi.[29]

Eventually, however, Adivasis—particularly the Gawda population—joined in large numbers in the protests against the American multinational Du Pont's project Nylon 6,6, which was to be set up in Keri's Bhutkhamb plateau. The police opened fire on the protesters in January 1995, killing a boy named Nilesh Naik and injuring an Adivasi girl, Ujwala Gawde, in the legs. The struggle was eventually successful; Nylon 6,6 pulled out of Goa and relocated its plant to Tamil Nadu. The success of the struggle was due to various factors, one of which was the forging of an alliance between the Adivasis and other settlers, including Dessais, that continued for almost a decade. However, the Adivasi rights issue was never brought up during the struggle, as the issue was tackled on purely environmental grounds—which cleverly concealed the various landed interests involved.

The same village rose again in revolt in 2007 when a Special Economic Zone (SEZ) was to be created on the same land. The village subsequently became a major centre for the wider protests that eventually led to scrapping of all 18 proposed SEZs in Goa.

Similarly, in the Meta Strips agitation in the late 1990s, it was pollution that was the main issue against this industrial plant at Verna in Salcete. The *Kunbis* residing in nearby villages were the main force in the protests, rallies and marches. The proposed plant site lay on their traditional grazing lands. Indeed, in case of accidents and disasters, it will be the nearby Adivasi villages that will be most affected

---

29. Movement against this Chemical Plant began in 2008, after a series of mergers it has come to be known as Syngenta.

both at the Ciba-Geigy plant in Corlim and at the Meta Strips site. The Adivasis have thus become industrial hostages.

Overall, however, those who are fighting the mining companies and industries are not paying adequate attention to reclaiming Adivasi lands. This is a first hurdle to the Adivasi rights struggle. The second is that, even if the Adivasis get the land back in their possession, there is no guarantee that mining will not be resumed; the mining leases will continue till they are cancelled by the state government.

5

Conclusion

In sum, the liberation of Goa in 1961 was in reality a liberation of the elites of Goa, who had taken over Adivasi lands during colonial rule. These elites have maintained and expanded the exploitative system founded during the Portuguese colonial regime and are busy selling off to real estate and pushing Adivasi communities to the margins. For the Adivasis, the struggle for liberation is just beginning and has a long way to go. They still have to find the way of linking up and forging alliances with the SC and OBC communities in this struggle.